AND
DYSLEXICS

by
Anne Henderson

1989

© Anne Henderson

ISBN 0-9512529-1-7

WEST GRID STAMP						
NN		RR	£195	WW		
NT		RT		WO		
NC		RC		WL		
NH		RB		WM		
NL		RP		WT		
NV		RS		WA		
NM		RW		WR		
NB		RV		W3		
NE						
NP						

Published by St David's College, Llandudno.
Typeset by Stiwdio Mei, Penygroes.
Printed by The Central Print Unit, UCNW, Bangor.
Jacket Cover and illustrations designed by Alan Holmes.

This book is dedicated to my father, Harry Stringman, who inspired many by his love of learning.

Anne Henderson has been teaching since 1961, working with pupils of all ages including adults. Since 1973 she has taught, peripatetically throughout Gwynedd, children with specific learning difficulties for the Dyslexia Unit at Bangor where Professor T.R. Miles was Head. In 1981 she began research for Professor Miles into maths and dyslexia and after four years she was invited to set up the Special Maths Department at St. David's College, Llandudno, where she still works. She lectures on maths and dyslexia all over the country to students, teachers and parents.

ACKNOWLEDGEMENTS

In order to write this book I needed much encouragement and this I got from my children Gareth and Bethan who have always had total belief in my teaching methods. I would also like to thank:

Prof. T.R. and Mrs E. Miles for their help, constant encouragement and enthusiasm.

Alan Waddon, Marion Horley, Ann Harrison, Eileen Stirling, Dorothy Gilroy and Alan Roberts for their views, ideas and help.

The Headmaster of St. David's College, Llandudno for his enthusiasm.

Ann Cooke and my colleagues at both the Dyslexia Unit, Bangor and and Cadogan Centre, St. David's College, Llandudno for sharing their thoughts with me.

Moira Thornton, my typist.

Finally, last but not least, my husband Gwyn for his endurance and coffee-making skills throughout this project.

CONTENTS

INTRODUCTION

Throughout my life I have always loved a challenge, so trying to help dyslexic pupils with mathematics was one I could not refuse. Since 1973 I had been working with language problems with children with learning difficulties, mostly dyslexics, and it was in 1981 when the challenge was given. My pupils had ranged in age from six to eighteen years but I had also done considerable work with the local Adult Literacy group.

The method of helping dyslexic pupils advocated by Professor T.R. Miles was the one used by the Dyslexic Unit at Bangor University, of which he was Head. His system of using a structured framework that was systematic and sequential was also flexible enough to allow personal teaching assets and expertise to be incorporated into each small step. Teaching in a multisensory way with long-term objectives and constant evaluation gave both my students and myself confidence, which in turn promoted learning. A one-to-one teaching situation needs a patient, understanding relationship between tutor and pupil, where both work in harmony to achieve educational aims. Teaching a dyslexic pupil to read and write needs many varied methods, pictures and mnemonics to emphasise and reinforce the logical small learning steps. In fact the more I worked with children with learning difficulties the more methods I seemed to find, for learning along with each individual pupil made lessons exciting for us both.

How was I to make mathematics lessons exciting?

At the beginning of my career in the early sixties I had been a 'Maths Teacher', but going back to it after so many years made me very apprehensive. In retrospect I need not have been so nervous, for I discovered that the very thought of maths puts fear into most adults, not just dyslexic pupils. The pupils had the extra problem of language difficulties, so mathematical language was causing just the same problems. In my ignorance I thought these difficult areas would be easy to spot but this was not the case. This book is designed to show some problems I encountered plus various methods which evolved from the teaching which has helped many of my pupils. The methods are ones which reflect my many years of experience working with dyslexic pupils in language. Throughout I have been aware that each pupil is an individual, and therefore various methods have been devised to make topics interesting. Topics too have been split into small logical steps, these often being different for each pupil. When some methods achieved success I tried them with other pupils and it is these 'tried and tested' methods that are included in the book — ones used during the last eight years when I've worked with dyslexic pupils on maths as well as with language. Every topic has a 'How to Help' section at the end with each point numbered for easy reference.

This book is deliberately 'small', for the simple reason that the sight of a 'thick' maths text book is a major source of fear to many people. It is designed to help both teachers and parents alike. For the latter, I want to say that I myself am a parent of a dyslexic child. As such I experienced the anguish and worry which all parents of dyslexic pupils know well. However this year my son Gareth attained an Upper Second Honours Degree from Liverpool University, and I feel his success should be included within this book to give some hope to others.

MAIN PROBLEMS
FEAR

'Mathephobia: Some people believe that the early settlers brought the disease with them although the disease was not recognised as such. Many people are carriers but escape in the usual medical check-ups perhaps because it is not a listed disease. A mother or father with mathephobia may inadvertently pass it on to their children by their negative attitude towards maths.'

Professor M. Sharma, (Framingham, Mass., USA)

This seemed to be present with most pupils once they realised they were to have an individual lesson in mathematics and before there had been time for a good teacher/pupil relationship to be formed. One child shook quite violently all through the lesson, whilst another fourteen year old pupil protested loudly. One teenager went white then just fainted quietly; I later discovered he had had difficulties with maths ever since he had 'learned' subtraction in the junior school and had never understood it. This failure in maths had affected all other areas of the curriculum and when he thought his 'weakest' area was to be discovered he fainted. One pupil aged nine became totally hysterical and lessons had to be abandoned.

It was not only pupils who showed fear. A Headmistress exclaimed, when the methods to be used were discussed, 'Please don't explain to me what you are going to do, just get on with it. It makes my palms go sweaty just to think about maths!' Very many young teachers have 'confessed' to me that they were dreadful themselves in maths, so liked to get lessons over as quickly as possible. In fact Professor Gulliford (1985) cites that the main problem encountered by the Cockroft Committee making their report 'Mathematics Counts', was to persuade people to participate, for there was widespread reluctance to be interviewed about mathematics even if it was described as arithmetic or just number. Approximately half the people approached would not participate and it was amazing how a simple piece of maths could induce feelings of anxiety, helplessness, fear and even guilt in people otherwise competent, qualified and successful in their own fields. Many of them said that they had never known or understood 'the proper method' to do maths problems and they had always felt their own way was 'just muddling through'.

HOW TO HELP

1. Establish a good relationship with the pupil — allow him to talk, laugh and relax and then each difficult area can be discussed freely without embarrassment (so important with an older pupil).

2. Use teaching games to start a lesson so that emphasis is not on the pupil but the game.

3. Use Information Technology, the computer and computer games as they are ideal to start informal discussions as well as allowing the pupil to show how good he is with modern technology.

4. Always emphasise his assets and things he can do well to boost confidence and allay fear.

POOR SHORT TERM MEMORY

Immediate recall of basic number facts is often an impossibility. Pupils forget the symbol they are using, such as addition, and change to another symbol, maybe subtraction, without knowing. Sometimes the computation will be correct for most of a problem and then suddenly a different process will be used and the calculation will be finished incorrectly. Almost all dyslexic students have difficulty with the verbal sequencing of tables, often giving an incorrect answer, pausing, giving another wrong answer and then trying to remember just what it is they were originally attempting to do.

HOW TO HELP

1. Discuss the symbol +, −, x, ÷ aloud, using language with which the pupil is familiar.

2. Talk about what the symbol means and the method involved, making sure the pupil is confident about the process.

3. Write down the symbol and highlight it with a colour to make it obvious and significant, so the pupil will constantly be aware of it.

4. With multiplication tables repeat the question aloud with the pupil so that its meaning is emphasised.

5. A teacher should constantly be aware of this short term memory problem, and therefore teach each pupil with an individual method most beneficial to that student.

ORGANISATION

General untidiness, badly spaced work, inky messy pages and illegible numbers seem to be the traits of most pupils with maths difficulties. Dyslexic pupils occasionally will start their work half-way down a page or even in extreme cases at the bottom right hand corner. They often number a problem badly so that in their confusion they include it within the 'body' of the computation on which they are working. Sometimes the pupil will be unable to 'decipher' his own work and will scribble over it, start again, make another mess, cross that out and start yet again. This performance can be repeated many times before the student is able to begin the mathematical process.

HOW TO HELP

1. Check that each pupil has equipment necessary for the lesson — pen, pencil, ruler, rubber, calculator and book.

2. Talk about the page size and where it would be best to begin.

3. Encourage use of rulers and columns to make calculation simple.

4. Encourage putting brackets around the actual number of the problem to isolate it from the main problem, or use a letter instead of a digit to identify problem.

5. Try to make a pupil responsible for the tidiness in his own book — encourage pride in a well kept book.

PROBLEMS WITH IDENTIFICATION AND DIRECTION

Pupils have difficulty deciding what kind of problem they have to solve. Sometimes especially with wordy written problems they cannot find what it is they are being asked to do. If students already have reading difficulties, then a written maths problem is double trouble! For not only does it require reading with understanding, but also means identifying a problem that needs to be solved. How often has a pupil said, 'But I can't see just what it wants me to do!'

Reading an actual number is difficult for pupils as often it requires positive identification of place values and decimal points. Sometimes, because they think nought values have no importance they ignore them or add them at will, so obviously this causes great confusion.

They might see   5002
say   52
or even   25
but record   205

With division for example:
see 64 ÷ 3
say 64 ÷ 3
write 64 ÷ 3
and do 3 ÷ 46
especially on a calculator.

Directional problems in maths are compounded because words and numbers are read from left to right, but addition, subtraction and multiplication calculations are worked right to left. However, division is done left to right. Two of my students do not like to do division from left to right. They have worked out a strategy that allows them to do division from right to left. Using this method they get accurate answers when dividing by 2 and approximate answers when dividing by other numbers, which they check on the calculator.

eg: **(a) 75 ÷ 2**
Working from the,right
5 ÷ 2 is 2.5
7 ÷ 2 is 3.5 x 10 = 35
35 + 2.5 = 37.5 This is correct.

(b) 362 ÷ 3
2 ÷ 3 = 0
6 ÷ 3 = 2 x 10 = 20
3 ÷ 3 = 1 x 100 = 100
Approximate answer = 120
Correct answer = 120.7

(c) 651 ÷ 4

1 ÷ 4 = 0

5 ÷ 4 = 1 x 10 = 10

6 ÷ 4 = 1.5 x 100 = 150

Approximate answer = 160

Correct answer = 162.8

HOW TO HELP

1. Allow pupil to read the question quietly to himself.

2. Read the question through with him.

3. Discuss what sort of a problem it is and what it is asking him to do.

4. Decide which mathematical symbol (+, - , x, ÷) is to be used. Write down the symbol and highlight it with a colour and discuss the method it implies.

5. Discuss direction possibly putting a 'direction arrow' to help.

6. Read the numbers involved aloud, discuss the decimal point, the comma signifying a thousand and place values of each digit.

7. If the student needs to copy a number use two pieces of card. Put one piece under the number to be copied and, when the number has been written down, put the other piece of card under the newly written number. Both numbers are then clearly identified, and the pupil can check for himself the accuracy of his copying.

8. Use of a tape recorder with instant playback is helpful in checking accuracy of copying.

Some numbers to practise with:

(a) 26	(b) 4.1	(c) 38.03
206	40.1	300.80
260	401	38,080
2,600.2	1,400.1	3,800.03
62,002.6	4,001.1	83,380.30

STRATEGIES

Younger pupils have not experienced failure too much or lost their confidence, but older pupils present greater problems. They have failed so often; they expect to fail and they will quickly tell you, 'I'm very thick!'. This situation needs careful handling, for by this time they will have devised their own strategies to cope and will not change an approach, in spite of seeing a better or quicker one. Sometimes I demonstrate another method but never insist on a particular way for them, as all confidence will be lost and we will be back to 'square one'. Strangely, long after these incidents a pupil may use an easier method I have demonstrated. He was obviously, therefore, acquiring knowledge and had been practising on his own, thus gaining confidence quietly; then when he felt able he incorporated the method into a problem. Never try to insist on a particular method, for they do 'close their minds' to anything new which threatens them and makes them feel insecure regardless of how slow their own method may seem.

SOME EXAMPLES OF STRATEGIES

Every strategy has been worked out individually by pupils and each has found the correct answer.

(a) Pupil aged 14 years

$$
\begin{array}{r}
218.89 \\
-171.32 \\
\hline
47.57
\end{array}
$$

$$
\begin{array}{r}
{}^1 2 \;{}^{10}\!\!\not{1}\; {}^{17}\!\!\not{8} . \;{}^{17}\!\!\not{8}\; {}^1 9 \\
-\; 1\; 7\; 1 . \; 3\; 2 \\
\hline
4\; 7 . \; 5\; 7
\end{array}
$$

|||||||||||||||||||IIIHH   19 – 2 = 17
7 down 1 to carry

|||||||||||||||||IIIHt   17 – 3 = 14 + 1 = 15
5 down 1 to carry

|||||||||||||||||IIIIIIIt   17 – 1 = 16 + 1 = 17
7 down 1 to carry

IIIIHHHt   10 – 7 = 3 + 1 = 4

The pupil said, 'I can see the problem immediately. It is where you have to take 7 from 1.' So he borrowed from the 2 in the hundreds column and 'passed down' a 1 from there to the 1/100th column. He then proceeded as above doing part subtraction and part addition to get the problem right.

(b) Pupil aged 12 years.

532
x 8

Think of 532 as 500
and 8 as 10
500 x 10 = 5000
8 is 2 lots of 500 less
5000 − 1000 = 4000

32
x8

I only know my 5 times table
5 x 8 = 40
So 40 doubled is 80 = 8 x 10
in 30 there are 3 tens

So 80 doubled is 160 = 8x20
160 + 80 is 240 = 8 x 30
2 x 8 = 16

4000 + 240 + 16 = 4256

(His teacher described David as 'thick and stupid', but after seeing
him solve this I decided he probably was a genius.)

(c) Pupil aged 10 years blushed when I asked her about subtraction and told me that she could only do subtraction if she thought about the problem in terms of eating apples.

So the calculation:

$$462$$
$$-287$$
$$\overline{}$$

became 462 apples and I have to eat 287. She kept putting up 10 fingers and then doing something strange, for she was taking the top row of numbers from the bottom. (Something I had always told my pupils not to do.) This then is the method she devised to eat her apples:

1. $$46\overset{1}{2}$$
    $$-2\underset{\llcorner}{8}7$$
    $$\overline{}$$

2 apples — I've got to eat 7. I can't do it. (She then put in two marks which she virtually ignored)

2. She then put 10 fingers up, and, counting from the 2 in the units column, she counted up to the 7 underneath it, and put down one finger each time she said a number. This left her with 5 fingers sticking up. 5 was put into the answer.

3. The she said, '6 apples and I've got to eat 8' (2 more marks were put in)

$$\begin{array}{r} 4^{|}62 \\ -^{|}287 \\ \hline \\ \hline \end{array}$$

4. She put 10 fingers up again and, starting with 6, she counted up to 8, which left her with 8 fingers sticking up. She then said, 'and 1 more' and she put down another finger, which left her with 7. 7 was put in to the answer.

5. To finish she said, '4 apples, eat 2 and 1 more leaves 1'. 1 was then put into the answer.

$$\begin{array}{r} 462 \\ -287 \\ \hline 175 \end{array}$$

The answer of 175 is correct.

OLDER CHILDREN

Obviously with older pupils gaps in existing knowledge have to be filled in carefully, then confidence will not be destroyed. By the time they reach adolescence many pupils have given up on maths and 'opted out' of the subject. Failing constantly in the past they no longer try to understand anything in a subject which they think is too difficult and complex for them.

HOW TO HELP

1. Form a good working relationship.

2. Discuss the 5 basic symbols of maths and the language used with them.

3. For each topic devise attack strategies designed specifically for every pupil. Strategies he understands and can work out for himself.

4. Reduce the strategies to key moves (like key words in language); then write them down and underline and highlight them with colour to give the pupil a good visual representation of each move.

MATHEMATICAL LANGUAGE PATTERNS

Chinese Proverb　What I hear — I forget
　　　　　　　　What I see — I remember
　　　　　　　　What I do — I understand

In language teaching I had always begun with the five vowels which were put in the first page of the pupil's book and were used constantly for reference. It became apparent that the five basic symbols in mathematics were comparable to the vowels, for at least one of them was used in every mathematical computation. As I always used visual circular planning for techniques in language a similar approach seemed ideal in maths; then the 5 mathematical patterns to evolve were as follows.

A.

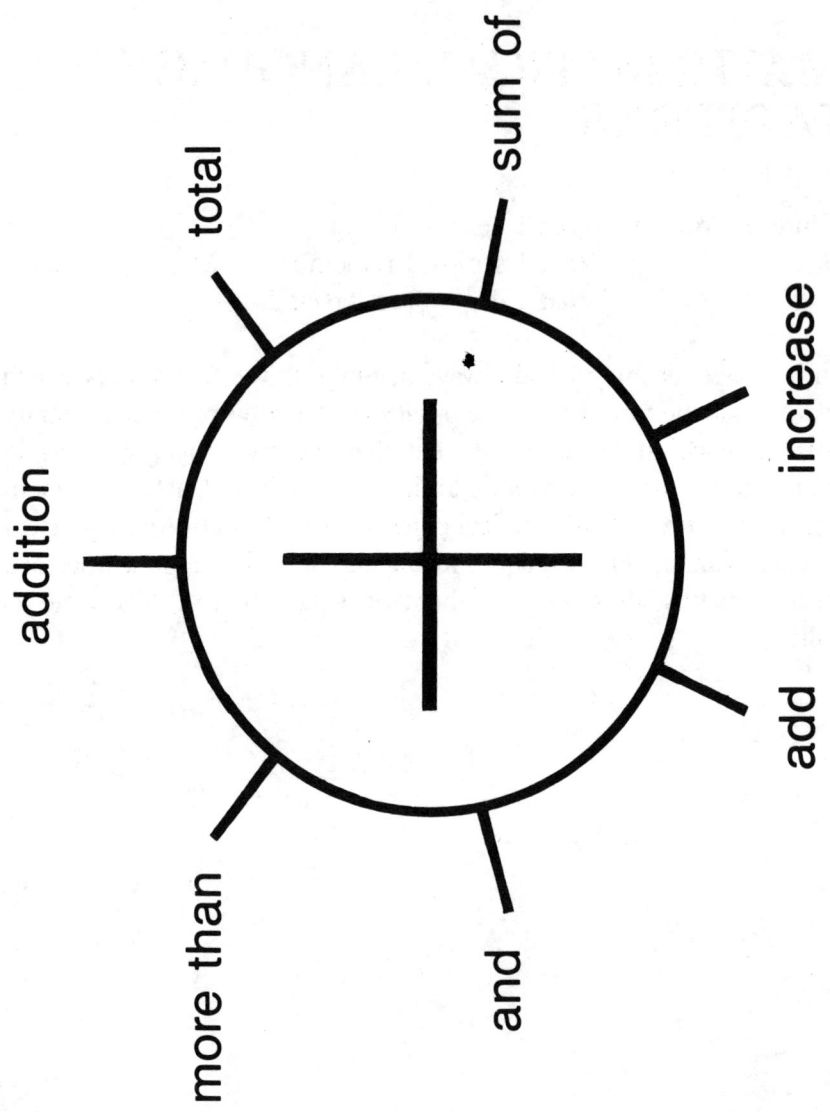

B.

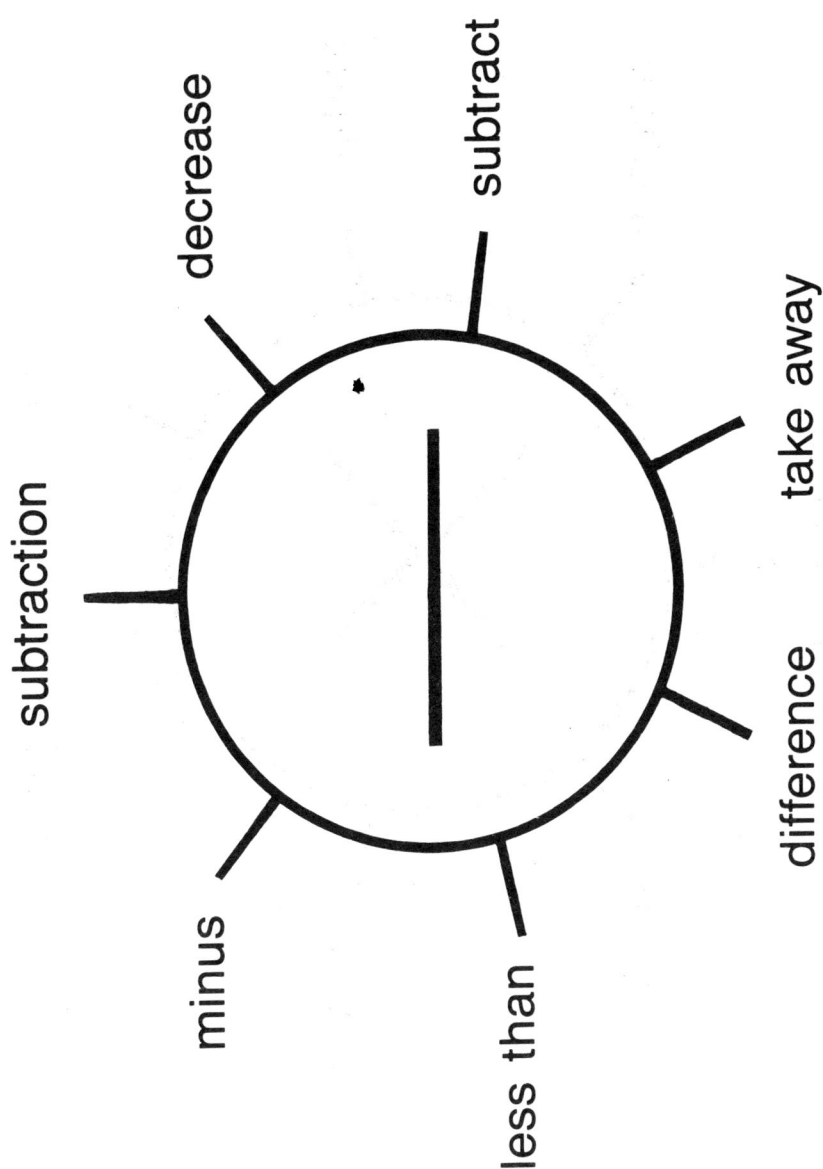

subtract

decrease

take away

subtraction

difference

minus

less than

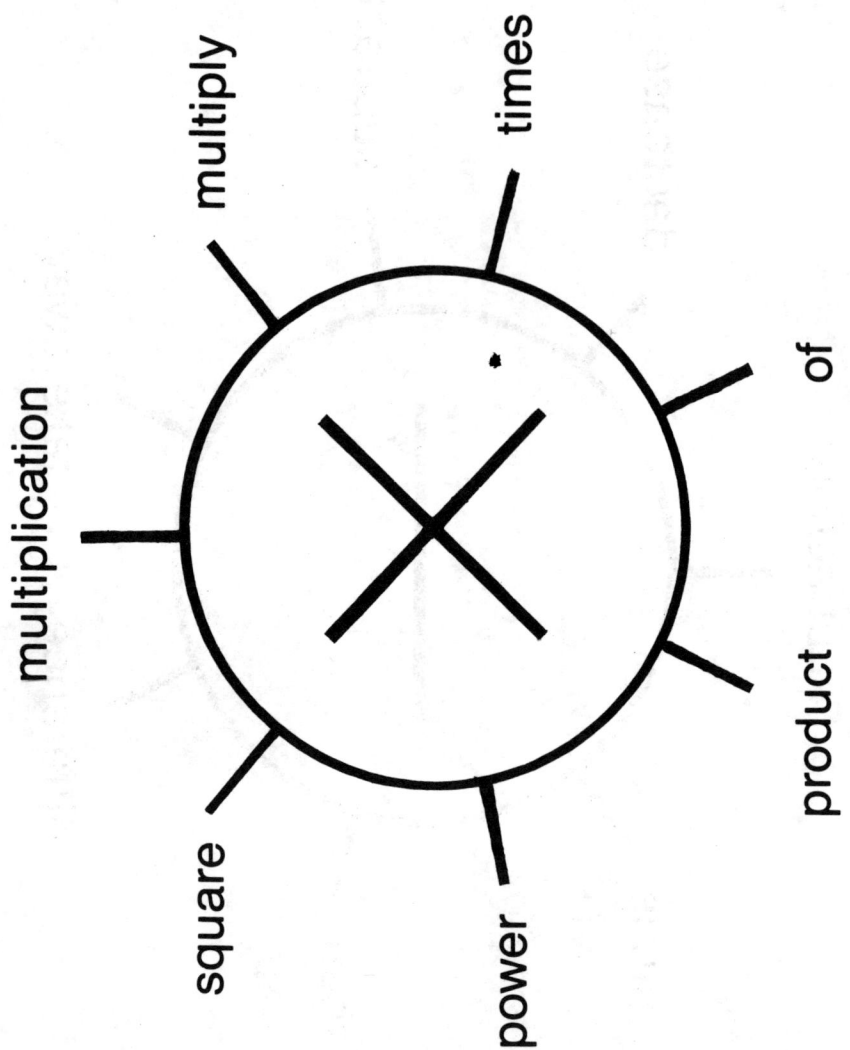

c.

D.

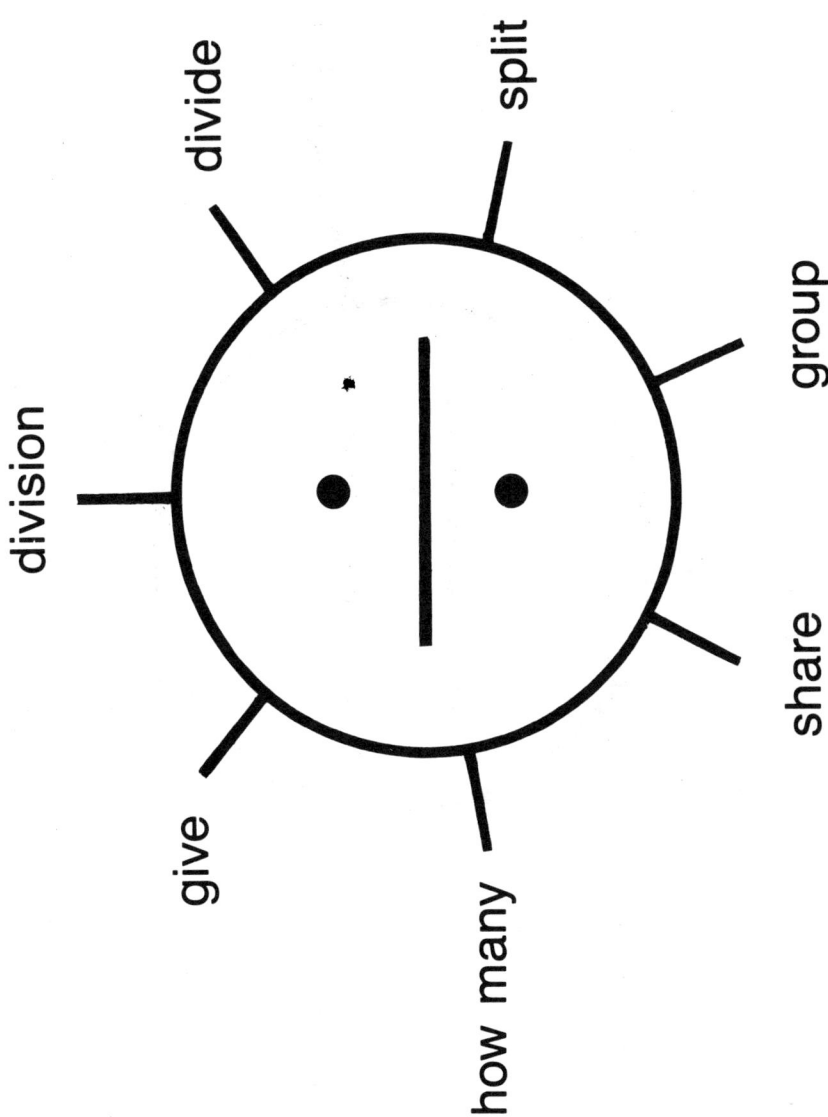

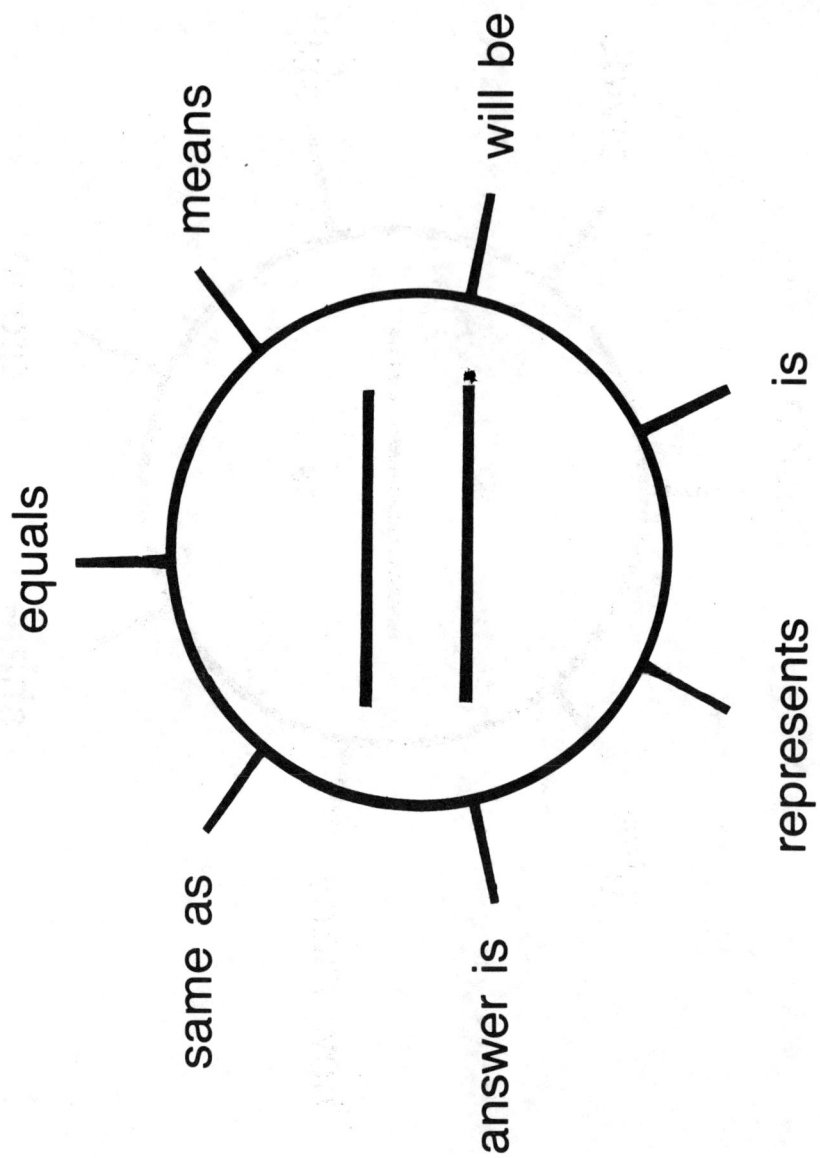

E.

After dealing with each symbol individually, I find it helpful to connect them up by putting them together on the same page. Discuss the similarity of + and x (slightly turned), and also of - and ÷ (just added dots).

Then putting them in the following pattern will connect them up visually.

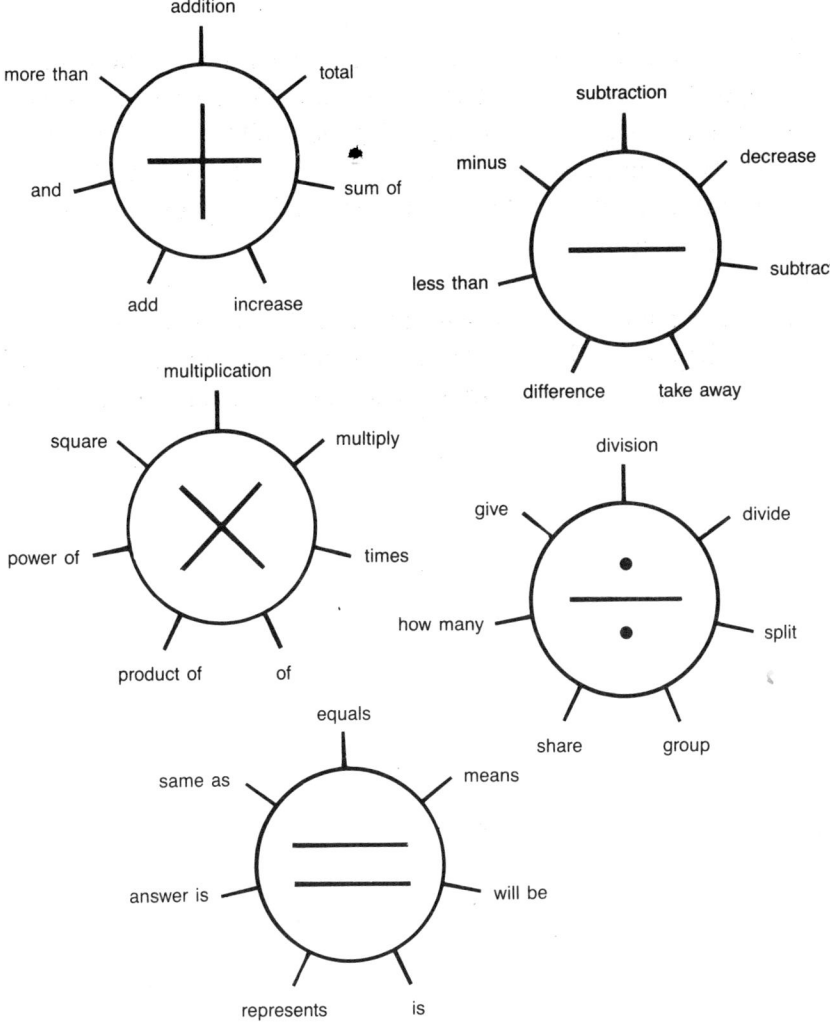

HOW TO HELP

1. Allow pupil to put in his own words.

2. Use concrete apparatus, Dienes blocks, Cuisinaire rods, Centicubes etc. to show what the symbol means. Trade with the apparatus, e.g. 'Give me 10 units for this ten stick' and do it physically not just orally.

3. Allow the pupil to use the apparatus regardless of how slow he is or the time taken. It is so easy for a teacher to demonstrate accurately that sometimes allowing the pupil to touch the apparatus seems a useless activity, especially if he continually uses it incorrectly. (We, as teachers, can forget that a pupil learns through his own errors.)

4. Use apparatus with which both you, the teacher, and the pupil are happy. (If the material is something a pupil has failed with many times he will not try to understand the method being shown).

N.B. APPARATUS

a. Cardboard cut into these shapes is useful and cheap.

b. The unit can be cut into 1/10ths and even 1/100ths.

c. The big red decimal point is an excellent teaching aid.

100   10   1   decimal point

$\frac{1}{10}$

$\frac{1}{100}$

HOW TO HELP WITH TABLES

1. With 1″ plastic squares build up tables pattern.

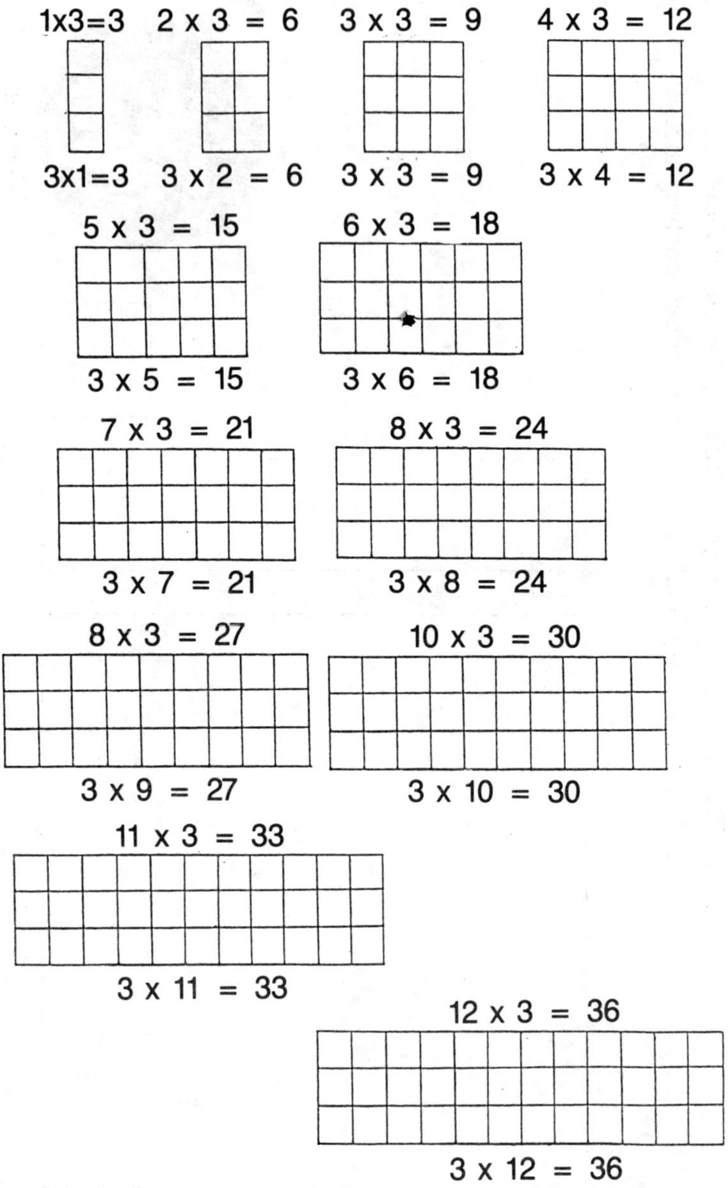

1x3=3   2 x 3 = 6   3 x 3 = 9   4 x 3 = 12

3x1=3   3 x 2 = 6   3 x 3 = 9   3 x 4 = 12

5 x 3 = 15   6 x 3 = 18

3 x 5 = 15   3 x 6 = 18

7 x 3 = 21   8 x 3 = 24

3 x 7 = 21   3 x 8 = 24

8 x 3 = 27   10 x 3 = 30

3 x 9 = 27   3 x 10 = 30

11 x 3 = 33

3 x 11 = 33

12 x 3 = 36

3 x 12 = 36

Table A

odd	even	odd	even	odd	even	odd	even	odd	even
1	2	3	4	5	6	7	8	9	10
11	12	13	14	15	16	17	18	19	20
21	22	23	24	25	26	27	28	29	30
31	32	33	34	35	36	37	38	39	40
41	42	43	44	45	46	47	48	49	50
51	52	53	54	55	56	57	58	59	60
61	62	63	64	65	66	67	68	69	70
71	72	73	74	75	76	77	78	79	80
81	82	83	84	85	86	87	88	89	90
91	92	93	94	95	96	97	98	99	100

THREE TIMES TABLE EXAMPLE (Table B)

odd	even	odd	even	odd	even	odd	even	odd	even
1	2	3	4	5	6	7	8	9	10
11	12	13	14	15	16	17	18	19	20
21	22	23	24	25	26	27	28	29	30
31	32	33	34	35	36	37	38	39	40
41	42	43	44	45	46	47	48	49	50
51	52	53	54	55	56	57	58	59	60
61	62	63	64	65	66	67	68	69	70
71	72	73	74	75	76	77	78	79	80
81	82	83	84	85	86	87	88	89	90
91	92	93	94	95	96	97	98	99	100

2   Give the pupil a 1 to 100 number square table A. Allow him to colour in the relevant numbers of the times table he is studying, such as table B. The pattern gives the pupil visual representation, to reinforce the learning process.

3. Listen to disco tables tapes.*

4. Discuss tables facts known well by the pupil and use them to work out more difficult ones

eg: (a) 7 x 7
use 5 x 7 = 35
then 2 x 7 = 14
so 7 x 7 = 35 + 14 = 49

(b) 8 x 9
say is the same as 9 x 8
use 10 x 8 = 80
then 1 x 8 = 8
so 8 x 9 = 80 – 8 = 72

5. Use fingers to do gypsy method for tables from 6 x 6 to 10 x 10.

*See page 66

Gypsy Method

eg. To do 7 x 8

(a) Make a bridge by putting the 7 from one hand to the 8 on the other hand. The bridge counts as 2 tens.

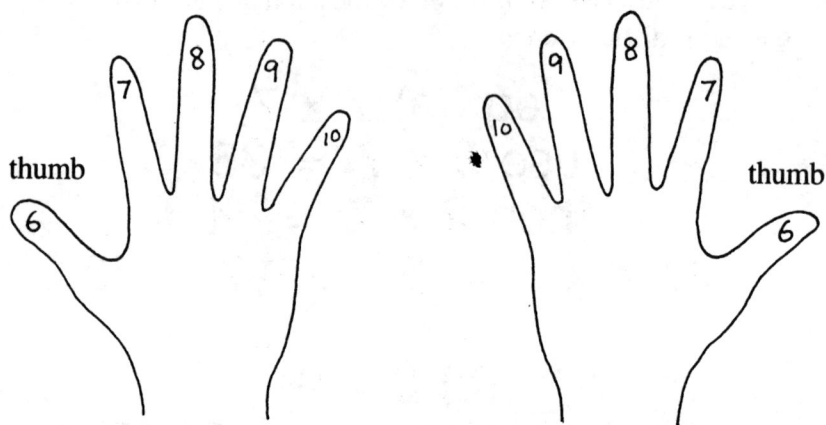

Each hand is numbered from 6 to 10 as in the above diagram.

(b) From the bridge the remaining fingers nearest to the body on both hands i.e. 3 are all tens in total, and 2 tens from bridge, 5 = 50.

(c) The fingers left over, 3 on one hand and 2 on the other, have to be multiplied together, 3 x 2 = 6.

Answer = 56

6. 9 x table can be taught with fingers.

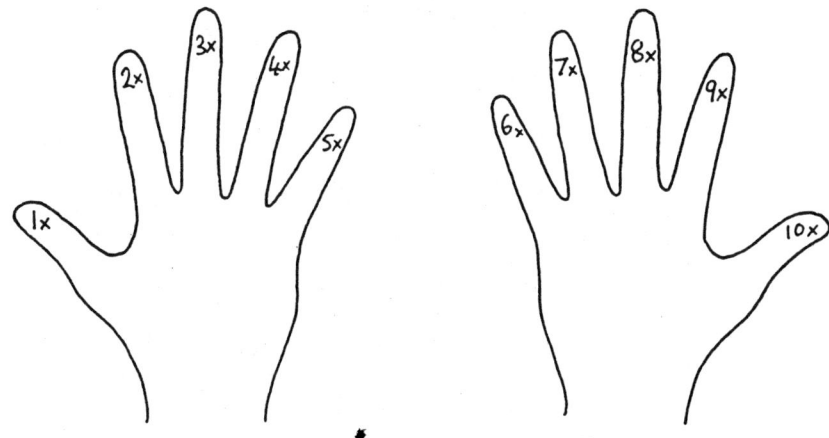

Method

1. To do 1 x 9 put down thumb on the left hand, the 9 fingers left are the answer.
2. To do 2 x 9 put down forefinger on left hand. The thumb to the left of the finger is now a ten and 8 remaining fingers.
3. To do 6 x 9 put down little finger on right hand. The answer is given by 5 fingers on left hand and 4 on right.

7. Table squares are useful. I usually give pupils three, all different sizes. The big one is to put onto the ceiling, the small one we stick on cardboard and the remaining one is stuck into the front of the book. (See Table C)

Table C

1	2	3	4	5	6	7	8	9	10	11	12
2	4	6	8	10	12	14	16	18	20	22	24
3	6	9	12	15	18	21	24	27	30	33	36
4	8	12	16	20	24	28	32	36	40	44	48
5	10	15	20	25	30	35	40	45	50	55	60
6	12	18	24	30	36	42	48	54	60	66	72
7	14	21	28	35	42	49	56	63	70	77	84
8	16	24	32	40	48	56	64	72	80	88	96
9	18	27	36	45	54	63	72	81	90	99	108
10	20	30	40	50	60	70	80	90	100	110	120
11	22	33	44	55	66	77	88	99	110	121	132
12	24	36	48	60	72	84	96	108	120	132	144
	2	3	4	5	6	7	8	9	10	11	12

1	2	3	4	5	6	7	8	9	10	11	12
2	4	6	8	10	12	14	16	18	20	22	24
3	6	9	12	15	18	21	24	27	30	33	36
4	8	12	16	20	24	28	32	36	40	44	48
5	10	15	20	25	30	35	40	45	50	55	60
6	12	18	24	30	36	42	48	54	60	66	72
7	14	21	28	35	42	49	56	63	70	77	84
8	16	24	32	40	48	56	64	72	80	88	96
9	18	27	36	45	54	63	72	81	90	99	108
10	20	30	40	50	60	70	80	90	100	110	120
11	22	33	44	55	66	77	88	99	110	121	132
12	24	36	48	60	72	84	96	108	120	132	144
	2	3	4	5	6	7	8	9	10	11	12

A FEW BASIC PRINCIPLES

Some basic principles have evolved during these years of working with dyslexics with maths. Initially I assumed they understood that noughts could be added after the decimal point but quickly realized I had thrown them into confusion. So the following are principles which I teach to all pupils and they themselves have told me how much they have been helped.

1. $1 = 1.0 = 1.00 = \dfrac{1}{1}$

$2 = 2.0 = 2.00 = \dfrac{2}{1}$

$3 = 3.0 = 3.00 = \dfrac{3}{1}$

2. In a fraction the line between the top and bottom number means divide.

$\dfrac{1}{2}$ means $1 \div 2 = 0.5$

$\dfrac{3}{4}$ means $3 \div 4 = 0.75$

The pupil can divide either with a pencil and paper or with a calculator to find out or check answer. The big red decimal point is useful to show in a concrete way the exact position of the decimal point within the numbers.

3. Using the 1″ squares to show

(a) odd and even numbers

1 on its own   2 a pair — even

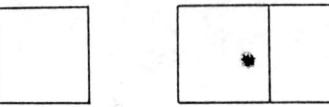

3 a pair and 1   4 2 pairs — even
on its own — odd

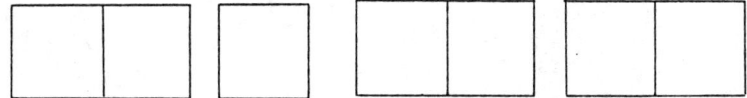

(b) square numbers (making squares)

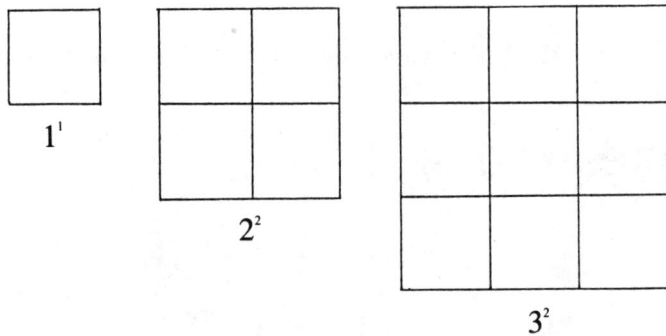

1^1

2^2

3^2

OTHER PROBLEMS
CALCULATORS

As calculators can be used in most examinations, it is essential that a student acquires proficiency in their usage. Whilst working with pupils with learning difficulties in maths, it became apparent that many of them were terrified of using a calculator. Usually they had failed so much with them they would go to any lengths to avoid using them by saying 'I've forgotten it', or 'It has broken'. I do think basic concepts have to be understood before a student can use a calculator properly, but often when I say, 'You can use your calculator', I've seen pupils quietly slipping them into their school bags hoping I haven't noticed. Many students have informed me that teachers had told them that they were cheating if they used a calculator, with the result that they avoided using them altogether. Pupils should use a calculator they are used to, but should be aware of the differences between various types of calculators.

HOW TO HELP

1. Use a calculator as much as possible, working with the pupil to give confidence. If both teacher and student have individual calculators, answers can be compared and checked for accuracy and important principles can be reinforced.

2. Allow the pupil to read numbers aloud from the calculator to show his understanding of decimal point and place value.

3. If the answer is constantly read incorrectly from the calculator, read on to a tape and play back to check (this helps a great deal).

4. Problems with the decimal point in money need practice, especially with reading the pence column eg. £26.2 on calculator read as 26 pounds 2p.

5. Watch for method used when doing division eg. 26 ÷ 3. Very often it is punched in as 3 ÷ 62 (reading from the right). Reading the question aloud, saying '26 divide by 3', helps when the pupil is using his calculator.

6. Make sure correct symbol key is used. Often a pupil will read the problem correctly i.e. 26 x 5, then do 26 + 5.

ESTIMATION

This is an exercise when an approximate result is obtained by rounding off numbers and using them instead of exact ones to find a 'rough' answer. Dyslexic pupils find this difficult to do, for if they have failed continually with correct values in problems, they lack confidence to use 'rounded off' numbers. Using a calculator accurately depends on a pupil's estimating skill, as it is easy for a dyslexic pupil to 'read' a value which bears no resemblance to the size of answer required eg: 1,000.63 might be read as 1.06. Estimation is a most useful technique to acquire as it develops a sense of awareness of size and quantity, vital in achieving a good understanding of number concepts. Predicting the size of an answer is just as important as working out the calculation accurately, for much of the number used in life is estimation, so it is important pupils are encouraged to develop this skill.

HOW TO HELP

1. Give a lot of practice from the very beginning so that the pupil will get into the habit of estimating first.

2. Use easy numbers to give a 'rough' answer eg: 43 use 40 or 97 use 100.

eg: (a) 43 + 97
use 40 + 100 Rough answer = 140

(b) 1.9 x 4.2
use 2 x 4 Rough answer = 8

(c) 41.06 ÷ 3.6
use 40 ÷ 4 Rough answer = 10

3. Round numbers up or down so the pupil loses his fear of estimation.

4. Talk about reasons for estimating and why it is important.

5. If a pupil constantly has problems with estimation put a £ sign in front of the amount and talk about 'I owe you £37, should I give you £30 or £40 if I round this to the nearest 10?' It is amazing how quickly they get the correct answer then!

6. With decimal places discuss the abbreviations 'dec.pl.' or 'd.p.' Do a drawing and write about the method.

| decimal point | 1st decimal place | 2nd decimal place | 3rd decimal place | 4th decimal place |

To correct a number to 1 d.p. LOOK AT the 2nd d.p.
If the number you are LOOKING AT is 5, 6, 7, 8, 9, you add one to the number. In the 1st d.p. (eg: Correct 1.879 to 1 dec.pl. is 1.9 for 7 in the second d.pl. is more than 5)

7. Significant figures, 'sig.fig.', 'S.F.' can also be shown initially by using large figures and the large decimal point. Often laughing about errors made in the size of the numbers makes the mathematical concept more acceptable and often remembered better.

eg: Write these numbers correct to 3 significant figures.

(a) 3547   (d) 0.08654
(b) 32,694   (e) 3.598
(c) 2.481   (f) 28.599

FRACTIONS

Fractions come a close second to learning multiplication tables for inducing fear. Pupils find the two adjectives that describe fractions 'improper' and 'vulgar' strange and not related to mathematical functions, and this adds to their confusion. Often other words used in connection with this topic equivalent, denominator and numerator are all difficult to say, write and understand. A fraction can describe a piece, part, group, length, area, percentage, number and size and is a difficult concept to grasp. However, once the basic concept is grasped and the pupil is able to do simple operations with the fractions most often used, viz. 1/4, 1/2 and 1/3, then I teach him how to use the fraction button on the calculator. One fourth former exclaimed when shown this button for the first time, 'Why have I wasted so much of my time doing complicated procedures to try and do fractions always unsuccessfully when I could have used a calculator? I could then have spent my time acquiring more vital skills in Maths.'

HOW TO HELP

1. Use many different concrete materials to demonstrate eg: chocolate, cake, string, apples, marbles and cardboard shapes.

2. Cut or divide into halves — talk about 'find a half', what are we doing? Cutting into 2 pieces. Devise a rule:-

   To find a half divide into 2 pieces (÷ by 2)

   A half (½) means 1 divide by 2.

3. Similarly to find a quarter (¼). Show concrete example.

   To find a quarter divide into 4 pieces (÷ by 4)

   A quarter (¼) means 1 divide by 4.

4. Talk and discuss thoroughly before 'writing down'.

5. Discuss why we need fractions and smaller pieces.
   (a) If shoes were bought only in whole sizes they would fall off.
   (b) Similarly if trousers could be bought only with metre waist measurements they would fall down.
   Using practical themes and having a great deal of discussion takes the fear out of the subject.

6. Watch out for reversals with fractions especially when doing subtraction.

7. Show pupil the fraction button on the calculator and allow him to practise. Experiment with the fraction button and then he can see for himself what to do.

8. Computer games with fractions make the concept more easily understood.

PERCENTAGE

As percentage is a term used throughout the world we expect pupils to understand it easily. Children with learning difficulties in mathematics have usually encountered the term many times in connection with school exams, prices in shops, cars and even holidays, and never understood it at all. If they never grasp the concept as they get older it becomes a major problem since it affects other areas of the curriculum, not just mathematics. Geography, Physics, Chemistry and many other subjects are influenced by their lack of understanding. Failing in percentage, therefore, means failing in these other areas too.

HOW TO HELP

1. Discuss the symbol %.
    % means ÷ (divide)
    and also % means /00 (one hundred)
    so % means $\div$ by 100

So 16% means 16 ÷ 100

2. 'Of' means x (from language patterns)
    So 16% of £40 means 16 ÷ 100 of £40
    0.16 x £40 (on calculator) = £6.40

3. To change something into a percentage do the opposite ie: x by 100
    eg: I get 17 out of 25 in an exam. What percentage have I got?

$\frac{17}{25}$ means 17 ÷ 25 = 0.68

So 0.68 x 100 = 68%

47

4. Discuss and practise often. Write the interpretation of the symbol (% means ÷ by 100) on cards, and then they can be stuck on to walls in kitchens or bedrooms, or put into pencil cases to be a constant reminder. (This method helps in language so I have incorporated it into maths teaching.)

5. Discussing approximations with regard to fractions is of great value.
   (a) How big is 50% of this piece of string?
   (b) Give me 25% of this piece of chocolate?
   (c) What is 75% of £1.
   Do many of these to give confidence.

6. 'Find VAT at 15%' is an exercise which they like to do because for the most part they can do it quickly without a calculator.
   (a) Find 10% (divide by 10). Record the answer.
   (b) Halve the answer written down.
   (c) Add both answers together.
   (d) Check on calculator.

7. With a new problem get the pupil to discuss exactly what he is required to do out loud. Decide on symbols to be used especially with regard to the % sign. Highlight the symbols and when he feels confident proceed.

8. Use a hundred square to connect up fractions, decimals and percentages. See table D.

Table D
FRACTIONS—DECIMALS—PERCENTAGES

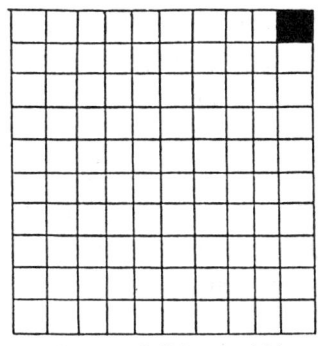

$$\frac{1}{100} = 0.01 = 1\%$$

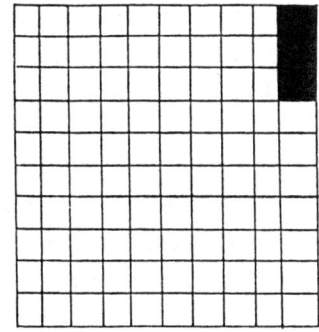

$$\frac{3}{100} = 0.03 = 3\%$$

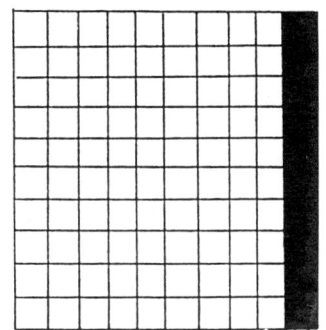

$$\frac{10}{100} = \frac{1}{10} = 0.10 = 10\%$$

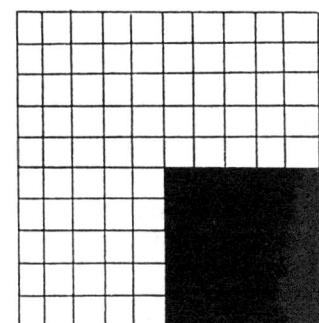

$$\frac{25}{100} = \frac{1}{4} = 0.25 = 25\%$$

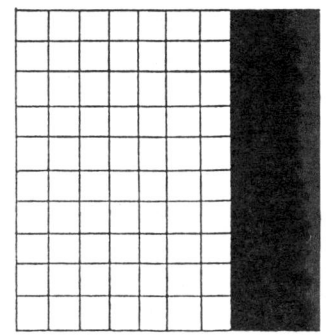

$$\frac{30}{100} = \frac{3}{10} = 0.30 = 30\%$$

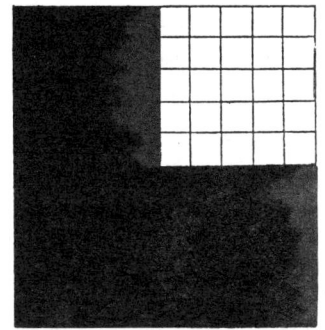

$$\frac{75}{100} = \frac{3}{4} = 0.75 = 75\%$$

TIME

Clockface to digital time or vice versa is the area that initially causes problems I find most pupils now with modern usage of information technology with digital diplays, are good with both 12 hour and 24 hour clock times. In fact my pupils are much better than I am at presetting a video recorder because they have grown up in a computer dominated age. Many travel timetables are written using the 24 hour clock so that pupils are used to reading times from 0000 hours (midnight) to 2400 hours (midnight again). Remembering the number of days in a month or year, or indeed how many weeks in a year, often causes difficulties.

HOW TO HELP

1. Give a pupil a card showing months and connecting numbers which he can keep in his pocket. (Especially good for adults dealing with official forms.)

1.	January	JAN	31 days
2.	February	FEB	28 days
3.	March	MAR	31 days
4.	April	APR	30 days
5.	May	MAY	31 days
6.	June	JNE	30 days
7.	July	JLY	31 days
8.	August	AUG	31 days
9.	September	SEP	30 days
10.	October	OCT	31 days
11.	November	NOV	30 days
12.	December	DEC	31 days

2. Use a cardboard clock with clear numerals that the pupil can manipulate himself.

3. Collect local timetables and look at them giving practice with reading them. Often there is more information in the 'notes' section concerning abbreviations which need discussing. Go through these carefully together.

4. T.V. programmes connecting up various items of interest encourage 'lengths of programmes' to be calculated.

5. Cooking, of interest now to both sexes, concerns accurate use of time if success is to be achieved. Exercises involving menus and cooking time are both enjoyable and useful.

6. Use time lines to work out passage of time. Students appear to prefer correcting the time at the beginning so that 'adding on' can be done in preference to 'taking off' at the end.

   eg:1 A T.V. programme begins at 7.35 and ends at 8.55. How long does it last?

   20 mins   1 hour

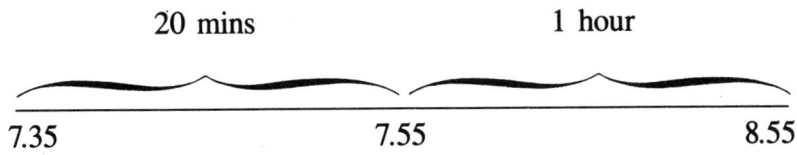

   7.35   7.55   8.55

   7.35 to 7.55 = 20 mins.
   7.55 to 8.55 = 1 hour.

   Time is 1hr 20mins.

eg:2 A train journey starts from London at 10.22 and arrives in Glasgow at 15.58. How long does the whole journey take?

36 mins	1 hr	1 hr	1 hr	1 hr	1 hr

| 10.22 | 10.58 | 11.58 | 12.58 | 13.58 | 14.58 | 15.58 |

10.22 + 36 = 10.58

Journey takes 5 hr 36 mins.

7. Using a similar line for distance helps. Seeing the problem instead of just thinking about it in words really helps.

eg: A journey from AB is 60 km. If a car is travelling at 45 kmph how long will the journey take?

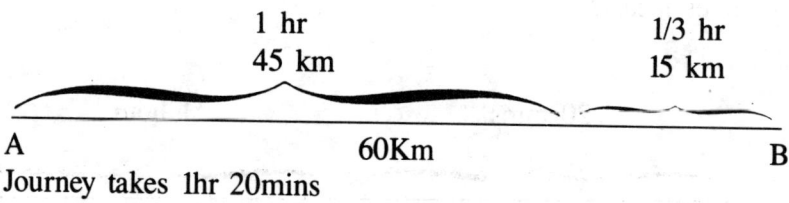

1 hr	1/3 hr
45 km	15 km

A   60Km   B

Journey takes 1hr 20mins

RATIO

The words and symbols used with this topic seem to have little relevance to the concepts involved. They do not indicate the action required and this makes pupils very confused. A ratio can be expressed as a fraction eg: If two numbers x and y are in the ratio 2:3, that means x is ⅔ the size of y. 2:3 can also be written ⅔ and it is this connection with 'fractions' that makes students very nervous as soon as the word ratio is mentioned.

The scale of a map compares the length on the map, to actual lengths on the ground, and is sometimes called a map ratio. Therefore, a scale of 1cm. representing 4 km. can be shown as 1 cm: 4 km. These two dots ':' cause much confusion and I have known some students ignore one dot and read the single dot left as a decimal point.

HOW TO HELP

1. Discuss abbreviations, language and symbols thoroughly.

2. Use illustrations to give a visual representation of the problem then it becomes meaningful. (I draw little stick people and always use bubbles as I would when planning an essay.)
   eg: £36 is divided between Bill, Jill and Sue in the ratio 4:3:2. How much does Jill receive?

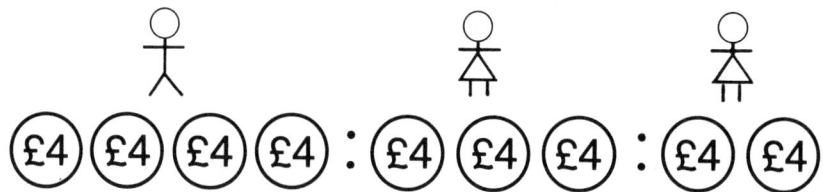

Seeing the bubbles the student realizes that the £36 needs splitting into 9 groups. So 36 ÷ 9 = 4. Each bubble is worth £4. He soon sees Jill will get £12. Once they understand this using problems with easy numbers students can soon deal with big numbers without the illustrations to help.

3. With map ratios, look at local maps of areas the student is familiar with, and talk about the distances involved. Pupils quickly understand the connection between the numbers given as the 'scale'.

4. Students with learning difficulties sometimes find it hard to connect activities, which they do in other subjects, to mathematics. Technical drawing, a subject in which they often excel, is directly concerned with scale drawings. Often, once this connection is pointed out, they quickly realise that map ratio is something in which they are good, and so this topic is no longer a problem.

PROPORTION

Quantities are described as proportional if they each change at the same rate, so that if one increases (or decreases) the other increases (or decreases) accordingly. Students find it difficult after reading a question, to decide what action to take. Often, there are other non-mathematical words they have to understand before they can grasp the meaning of the problem.

eg: This recipe shows the ingredients required for Welsh Rarebit. Write down the quantities if 12 ounces of cheese are to be used.

2 Tbs milk
1 Tsp flour
Pinch of mustard
4 oz cheese

The words ingredients, Welsh Rarebit and quantities are difficult to read and understand. Abbreviations given in the recipe are sometimes ones they are not familiar with, and so they spend much time trying to work out their meaning. It is only then they can get down to solving the problem.

Quantities that increase at opposite rates can be described as being inversely proportional, so that if one is halved then the other is doubled.

It is this property with the topic that confuses a child with learning difficulties. Often, especially if he is anxious, he will halve both quantities or double both, because he has forgotten exactly what the question was asking him to do.

HOW TO HELP

1. Read question through and decide what sort of problem it is (inverse or direct proportion).

2. Talk about the symbols shown in the problem, and what they mean. Make sure the student understands the language involved.

3. Once the course of action is decided, draw the problem out pictorially. This visual method helps clarify the situation.

   eg: It takes three men three hours to empty a furniture van. One of the men trips and hurts his leg before starting the job. How long will it take the two remaining men to empty the van? (Will it be more or less time?)

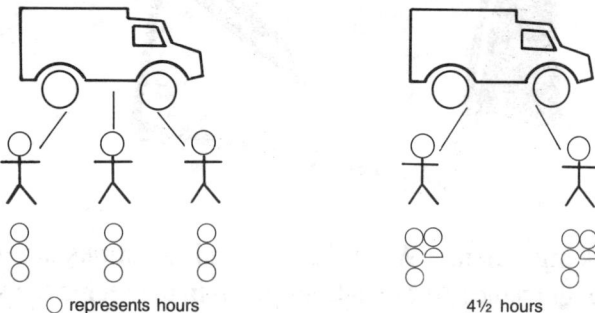

O represents hours   4½ hours

The picture shows that nine hours are needed to empty the van. So with just two men it will take 4½ hours.

4. Once understanding and success is achieved confidence grows and the pupil will be able to use the same attack strategy applying it to other questions and situations.

ALGEBRA

The name of the topic plus the fact that letters and numbers are used together causes much distress. Obviously with pupils experiencing difficulties with symbols this whole topic is filled with hazards. Some pupils, once the basic principles have been discussed, grasp the total concept quickly and easily. Many others need to be taught in minute stages, sometimes experiencing learning 'steps' where I have failed to see any! It is essential with these pupils to make sure each step taken is very small; for if it is too big the pupil will be lost and the purpose of the tuition is wasted. Should this happen then steps must be retraced either to the beginning or to where the pupil is confident: one can then proceed slowly from there. Whether to go back to the beginning or to the confidence spot depends on the pupil and the teacher's assessment of the pupil's methods.

HOW TO HELP

1. Talk through the basic concepts involved. I try to use concrete aids such as scales or a balance to show the meaning of the equals sign. I even use building blocks and stick letters onto them to demonstrate the meaning of 3x ie:

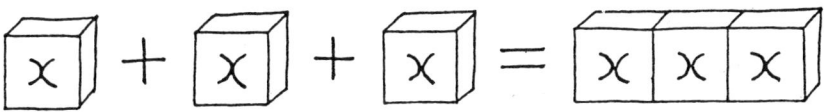

2. Letters or letters and numbers close together mean there is a multiplication sign between them.

ie: 1a means 1 x a
ab means a x b

3. If a letter is used without a positive or negative sign attached to it then always understand +1 to be there.

ie: x = +1x
a = +1a

4. The + (add) and x (multiply) as explained earlier mean the same thing (they are just written slightly different).

ie:
3a means (3 x a) means +1a +1a +1a
4b means (4 x b) means + 1b + 1b + 1b + 1b
4b – b is not 4
(b + b + b + b) – b = 3b
4b – 1b = 3b

5. Point out that the sign - or + to the left of the digit or letter is the one that belongs to it. (Dyslexics often confuse left and right, so in algebra connect up the letter with the sign that follows it!)

TRIGONOMETRY

The main problem with this topic is the use of right angled triangles. This was highlighted with a fifth former who presented me with the question:

A and B are points on two mountains. Find the distance between them using Pythagoras' rule.

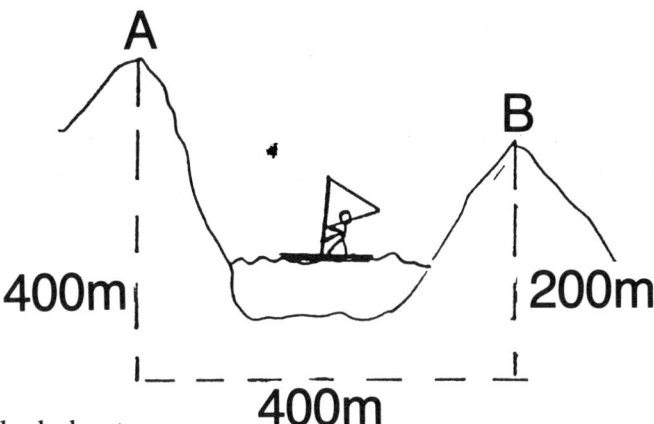

We talked about
Who was Pythagoras? What was his rule?
What is a right angled triangle?
Student answered

'A right angled triangle is one with 90° on the right. A triangle with 90° on the left is a left angled triangle.'

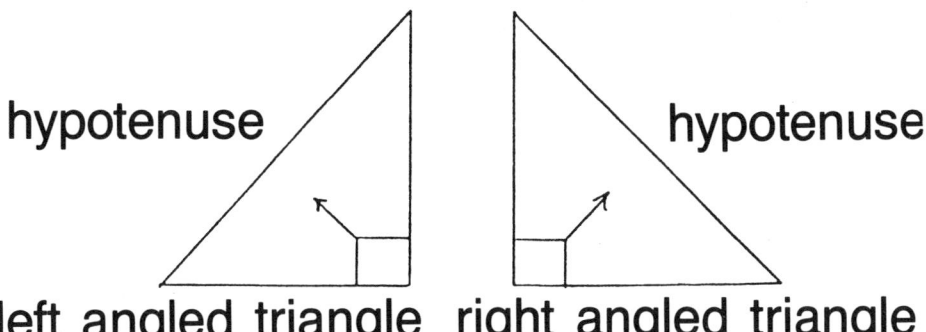

HOW TO HELP

1. Draw in the right angle first.

2. Indicate with an arrow the hypotenuse.

3. Discuss which sides are adjacent and which are opposite. This seemingly simple item can take a great deal of time as dyslexics cannot connect up angles and lines easily. Often they do it but forget as soon as they start to apply a theory.

4. Once the mnemonic Soh Cah Toa is explained they can apply it (Mathematical theorists do not like this method but it is the only one I have used which has any success.)

    Soh means $Sin = \dfrac{opposite}{hypotenuse}$

    Cah means $Cos = \dfrac{adjacent}{hypotenuse}$

    Toa means $Tan = \dfrac{opposite}{adjacent}$

5. Practical applications with many examples seem to help and certainly give a pupil confidence to try and solve a problem instead of giving up.

PROBABILITY

This is a good topic to teach which pupils really enjoy whether it is spinning a coin, tossing a die or pulling coloured marbles out of a bag. (In a short space of time they become far quicker than me at finding answers.)

HOW TO HELP

1. Use concrete apparatus to teach the concept, such as marbles, coins, playing cards.

2. Incorporate their keenness especially with pupils having difficulties with basic concepts and ideas to teach eg: odd, even, prime numbers. Put papers with numbers from 1 to 20 in a bag and ask, 'What is the probability of pulling out an even number?' Then even numbers have to be discussed and understood before an answer to the question can be found. (Especially good with difficult adolescents experiencing difficulties at a basic level.)

3. Use dice to teach number bonds whilst teaching concepts of probability.

4. Nets for dice can be made so reinforcing many mathematical concepts.

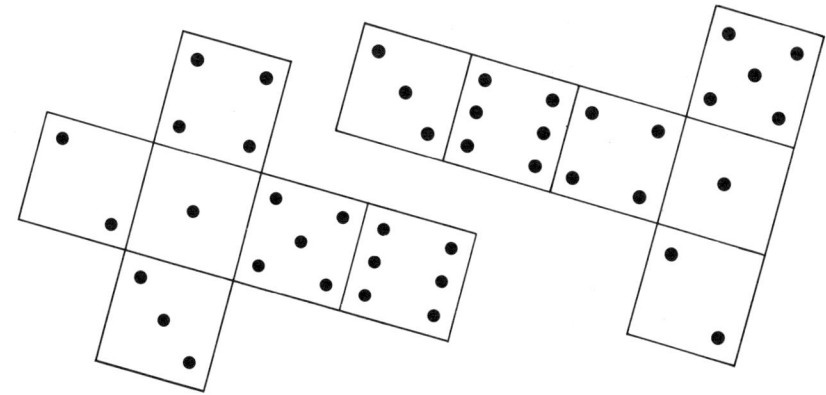

CONCLUSION

Throughout the whole period of mathematical tuition always interlink each lesson by overlapping knowledge taught in previous lesson. As often as possible discuss the connection between the four basic rules; also talk about prime numbers, factors about prime numbers, factors and mathematical terminology to familiarize pupil with this vocabulary and remove fear. If possible try to relate problems to something the pupil is familiar with; then better understanding is attained.

Treating each pupil as an individual with different problems and giving him his own personal attack strategy, has proved most rewarding. Seeing a student gain in confidence, achieve success and lose fear of the subject has been a bonus making this part of my career extremely satisfying. In fact approaching maths in this way has proved to make it enjoyable and indeed exciting. Many pupils have expressed their enjoyment of the subject, some wanting to take 'A' level mathematics so their fear of the subject has gone. To conclude I have summarized methods used into the following notes.

MATHS AND THE DYSLEXIC CHILD

1.   A dyslexic child is often good orally but not always. He usually can cope well with verbal problems. A teacher may, however, think he has not got a problem because of his seeming fluency.

2.   Number bonds both addition and subtraction cause problems so need practise.

3.   Tables cause problems. Several methods of helping in this area:
     a) finger tables
     b) tape, ie tables to music
     c) use of table square

d) calculator practice

e) table patterns

Almost all students with maths learning difficulties ask for help in this area as they feel this is where they are weak.

4. Mathematical language often causes problems, therefore much work needs to be done in this area, i.e. suitable text books. Rephrasing of questions etc.

5. Symbols again present severe difficulties to the dyslexic child so much help is needed in this area.

6. Short term memory usually causes much confusion, i.e. the student forgets halfway through whether to + or -.

7. Almost all dyslexics are poor in organisational techniques and therefore they need to be shown slowly and clearly, i.e. one step at a time.

8. Difficulties with direction need sorting out with verbal practice of up, down, right, left, before, after etc.

9. Concrete aids should be used wherever possible and then the pupil can use them and experience for himself the problem before recording.

10. Many pupils between the ages 11-17 have already developed compensatory techniques which work well on a simple level but tend to break down when more complicated material is met. We, therefore, need to form an 'easy' relationship with the pupil, so that he is able to discuss freely without embarrassment, his problems in Maths, however simple. After listening and watching we will then be in a position to offer help.

11. At all times care should be taken to build up the pupil's self-confidence, progress to the next step only when he has grasped the initial concept and at all times try to help with each 'step' of the calculation (no matter how small or simple) until the pupil feels able to cope with that particular operation himself.

12. Teaching should be:
systematic
sequential
structured — to the child's personal needs with frequent evaluation so methods can be adjusted if learning is not taking place.

SUGGESTED READING LIST

Ashlock, R.B. Error Patterns in Computation. 2nd Edition. Columbus, Charles E. Merrill, 1982.

Bath, Chinn and Knox (Eds.) Dyslexia Research and Its Application to the Adolescent (Edington School, The Chatauqua Academy 1984).

Burge V. Dyslexia, Basic Numeracy. Helen Arkell Dyslexia Centre, 1986.

Cockcroft W.H. Mathematics Counts. London, HMSO, 1982.

Floyd A. (Ed.) Developing Mathematical Thinking. London: Addison Wesley, OUP, 1981.

Gulliford R. 1985. Teaching Children with Learning Difficulties. Windsor, NFER, Nelson.

Holt J. 1982. How Children Fail Reading. Cox and Wyman.

Hornsby Dr B. 1984. Overcoming Dyslexia. London, Martin Dunitz.

Miles T.R. 1983 Dyslexia, The Pattern of Difficulties. Suffolk, Granada.

Stirling E.G. 1985. Help for the Dyslexic Adolescent. Bath, Better Books and St. David's College.

Sharma M.C. (Ed.) Focus on Learning Problems in Mathematics (all volumes). Center for Teaching/Learning and Mathematics, Framingham, Massachusetts.

BOOKS FOR PUPILS

One Minute Maths Books 1-8 (Altmans & Dent), Blackwell

Calculator Maths (K. Tyler), Blackie

Peak Maths Books 4-7 (A. Brighouse), Nelson

Mathswise Books 1-3 (R. Allan and M. Williams), Oxford

Mathematics Books 1-3 (M. Ashcroft), Letts Study Aids

GCSE Mathematics (R.C. Solomon), D.P. Publications Ltd

Dictionary of Maths (M. Brayton), J. Brodie Ltd

The 4 Rules of Decimals (K. A. Hellse), Longman

The 4 Rules of Number (K. A. Hellse), Longman

The 4 Rules of Metric, Measure and Time (K. A. Hellse), Longman

Investigating Numbers (Catherall), Wayland

TABLES TAPES

Tables. Disco. Webucational, Wimborne, Dorset.

Multiplication Tables. Cadence Cassettes, Totton, Southampton.

GAMES

	Supplier
Angle Race	E. J. Arnold
Area Dominoes	Taskmaster Ltd
Balance	E.S.A.
Calculator Lotto	Taskmaster Ltd
Cuisenaire Rods	The Cuisenaire Co. Ltd
Decimal Place Value Dominoes	Taskmaster Ltd
Decimal-Fraction Dominoes	Taskmaster Ltd
Equality	Peter Pan
Equivalence Playing Cards	Taskmaster Ltd
Fraction Dominoes	Taskmaster Ltd
Geometry	Taskmaster Ltd
Mathematical Language Patterns	Taskmaster Ltd
Name the Symbol Dominoes	Taskmaster Ltd
Shut the Box	M.B. Games
Table Shapes	Taskmaster Ltd
Time Dominoes	Taskmaster Ltd